Speak Spanish Today!

A conversation course on cassette for visitors to Spain

Hugo's Language Books Limited

This edition
© 1987 Hugo's Language Books Ltd
All rights reserved
ISBN 0 85285 117 0

Written by

Isabel Cisneros

3rd Impression 1991

Facts and figures given in this book were
correct when printed. If you discover any
changes, please write to us.

Printed in Great Britain by
Buckland Press Ltd, Barwick Road,
Dover, Kent

Preface

How many people have gained a background knowledge of Spanish yet still find themselves floundering in a Spanish shop or any other situation where they have to say a little more than 'How much is it?' and 'Thank you'? Are you one of those who has been through a home study or classroom course in the language but still cannot master the conversational element as easily as you had hoped?

The twelve conversations on this cassette recording are designed to bridge that gap. They assume a fair knowledge of Spanish grammar, but all are applicable to the everyday situations in which the visitor to Spain is most likely to find him- or herself . . . buying food or clothes, ordering meals, asking for directions and so on.

An effort has been made to keep the language colloquial, corresponding to what one actually hears in Spain, and so contracted forms and conversational turns of phrase have been used by the native Spanish speakers on this recording. The content of each dialogue, while remaining realistic, has been carefully devised to provide the learner with plenty of practical information about the Spanish way of life, especially in cases where it differs from our own.

Contents

Introduction

How to use the Course

Each conversation has been recorded twice. First, you will hear the speakers talking at a normal rate; listen to one of these complete conversations several times before progressing to the second rendering. In this, there is a pause before the visitor's part in the dialogue—giving you time to say the words yourself before hearing them on the tape. You can do this either by working from memory or by reading the part from the text.

To make it clear which part is the visitor's, we have indicated this in the text by the symbol • against each appropriate entry. This is especially necessary in those dialogues where several characters join together in conversation and an arbitrary decision has been made as to which must be the 'visitor'.

You may wish to record yourself on another tape and then compare your pronunciation with that of the original speaker; this will give you practice in both formulating what you want to say and understanding what is said to you in reply.

The notes and English translation

The notes are intended to make your stay in Spain easier and more enjoyable by drawing your attention to certain Spanish customs, as well as to linguistic features. Each marginal number in the Spanish conversation refers to italicised words in the following sentence; these are explained at the end of the piece, under *Explicaciones*. Try to understand these Spanish notes first, before referring to the English version under the heading *Notes*. You will see that these follow directly, instead of coming after the English translation of the conversations. The reference numbers are shown only in the Spanish dialogues because the notes often refer to a feature which has no equivalent in English.

The English translations of the conversations appear at the end of the book; these are as literal as possible, but we have given a free translation where a literal one would sound strange to the English ear.

Care of your cassette
Just in case you've forgotten how carefully a tape needs to be handled, here are some gentle words of warning! Do not switch your player from "play" to "rewind" or "fast forward" without stopping the tape first of all, and ensure that there's no slack tape between the two holes of the cassette before you insert it into your player. If there is, the tape may double back and become stretched, crumpled or broken by getting wound round the machine's capstan. To avoid this, simply insert a pencil (preferably one with flat sides) or your finger into one or other of the holes and turn the sprocket in the appropriate direction to take up the slack between the two hubs. Do not over-tighten the tape, for obvious reasons!

En el hotel

RECEPCIONISTA	Buenos días, señor. ¿En qué puedo servirle?
• CLIENTE	Buenos días. ¿Tiene Vd. una habitación individual para esta noche?
RECEPCIONISTA	¿Una noche nada más?
• CLIENTE	No, dos noches.
RECEPCIONISTA	Un momento, por favor, voy a mirar. Sí, señor, puedo ofrecerle habitación. ¿La quiere Vd. con baño o con ducha?
• CLIENTE	¿Qué precio tienen las habitaciones?
RECEPCIONISTA	La individual con ducha mil ochocientas, con baño dos mil quinientas pesetas.
• CLIENTE	1 ¿Está incluído *el desayuno*?
RECEPCIONISTA	Sí, señor. ¿Le interesa?
• CLIENTE	Sí, déme Vd. la habitación con ducha.
RECEPCIONISTA	2 Bien. Puedo darle la habitación trescientos doce en el tercer piso. El ascensor está al fondo del vestíbulo. ¿*Me deja el pasaporte* por favor? En seguida se lo devuelvo.
• CLIENTE	Tome Vd. ¿Sirven comidas en el hotel?

7

RECEPCIONISTA	Sí, señor. Tenemos un restaurante que está abierto de una a cuatro de la tarde y de ocho a once de la noche. También hay una cafetería abierta todo el día desde las ocho de la mañana hasta las doce de la noche.
• CLIENTE	Muy bien, gracias.
RECEPCIONISTA	¿Tiene Vd. el equipaje?
• CLIENTE	Sí, en el coche. Lo he tenido que aparcar a una manzana de aquí porque no había sitio delante del hotel.
RECEPCIONISTA	Tenemos garaje, así que puede Vd. traer el coche y el mozo le esperará a la puerta para coger el equipaje.
• CLIENTE	3 Entonces, ahora voy a buscarlo. ¿Puede Vd. decirme si hay *un banco* por aquí cerca? Necesito cambiar dinero.
RECEPCIONISTA	Tiene Vd. un banco a unos quinientos metros de aquí. Tuerza Vd. a la derecha al salir del hotel. El banco está en esta misma acera.
• CLIENTE	Bien, gracias. Ahora vuelvo.

Explicaciones

1 En ciertos hoteles no sirven el desayuno en las habitaciones. Hay que bajar a tomarlo en el comedor.

2 En todos los hoteles hay que rellenar un impreso con los datos de filiacion de cada persona y numero de pasaporte.

3 Los bancos estan abiertos de ocho de la mañana a dos de la tarde, de lunes a viernes. Los sabados abren a las ocho de la mañana y cierran a la una de la tarde.

Notes

1   Some hotels do not serve breakfast in the bedrooms, only in the dining room.
2   In all hotels one has to fill in a registration form with details of name, home address, and passport number.
3   Banks are open Monday to Friday from 9 a.m. to 2 p.m.; Saturdays from 9 a.m. to 1 p.m.

En la cafetería

• CARMEN		¿Dónde nos sentamos en una mesa o en la barra?
PILAR		Yo creo que es mejor en una mesa. Los taburetes de la barra no son muy cómodos.
• CARMEN		Es verdad. Vamos a esa mesa al lado de la ventana.
CAMARERO		Buenas tardes, señoritas. ¿Qué desean tomar?
• CARMEN		¿Qué tienen para comer?
CAMARERO	1, 2	Tortitas, *sandwiches*, *pepitos*, perritos calientes . . .
• CARMEN		Yo quiero tortitas con nata y un café con leche en taza grande.
CAMARERO		¿Cómo quiere las tortitas, con caramelo, chocolate o fresa?
• CARMEN		Con caramelo, por favor.
CAMARERO		Bien. Y Vd. señorita, ¿qué va a tomar?
PILAR	3	A mí tráigame un perrito caliente y un *Cuba libre*.
		. . . .
• CARMEN		¿Dónde están los servicios, por favor?
CAMARERO		Por esa puerta del fondo.
• CARMEN	4	Gracias. ¿Hay *teléfono público*?
CAMARERO		Sí, al lado de la puerta de los servicios.
• CARMEN		¿Puede Vd. cambiarme un billete de cien? No tengo dinero suelto para el teléfono.

10

CAMARERO	Sí, señorita. ¿Cómo lo quiere?
• CARMEN	Deme una moneda de cincuenta, una de veinticinco y el resto en monedas de duro, si es posible.
CAMARERO	Aquí tiene Vd.
• CARMEN	Gracias. Ahora vengo, Pilar.
PILAR	¡Vale!

Explicaciones

1 Los sandwiches se sirven siempre tostados; si se quieren sin tostar hay que advertirlo.

2 Un pepito es una barra de pan pequeña con un filete de ternera entre medias.

3 Un Cuba libre es una Coca-Cola con ron o ginebra.

4 En los teléfonos públicos se utilizan monedas de cinco (duros), veinticinco o cincuenta pesetas. Se puede llamar directo a toda España y gran parte del extranjero. La mayoría de los teléfonos públicos tienen una lista con los prefijos de las distintas regiones españolas y de los países extranjeros.

Notes

1 Sandwiches are always served toasted; if you want them made with fresh bread you have to ask the waiter.

2 A *'pepito'* is a veal steak sandwiched between two sides of a small baguette loaf.

3 A *'Cuba libre'* is rum and coke; the same name is given to gin and coke, which is becoming increasingly popular in Spain.

4 In public phones coins worth five, twenty-five or fifty pesetas are used (fives are colloquially called *'duros'*). One can call direct to anywhere in Spain and most countries abroad. Most public phones have a list with the code numbers of the various regions in Spain and in foreign countries. To phone England dial 07 44 followed by the STD code (leaving out the 0 in front of that code).

En el restaurante

CAMARERO		Buenos días, señor. ¿Una mesa para dos? Vengan por aquí.
• SR. SÁNCHEZ		Mientras elegimos, ¿puede Vd. traernos una cerveza y un vermut, por favor?
CAMARERO		Ahora mismo se los traigo. ¿Desean Vds. algo para picar?
• SR. SÁNCHEZ		Sí. Tráiganos usted unas aceitunas rellenas y unos calamares fritos.
CAMARERO	1, 2	Muy bien. Aquí tienen Vds. la carta. *El cubierto del día* es muy bueno. Puedo recomendárselo. Hay *fabada.*
• SR. SÁNCHEZ		(a su mujer) ¿Qué te parece? ¿Tomamos el cubierto?
SRA. SÁNCHEZ		No me gusta el cubierto de hoy. Prefiero comer a la carta.
• SR. SÁNCHEZ		Sí, yo también.

....

CAMARERO		Aquí tienen sus aperitivos. ¿Han decidido ya lo que van a tomar?
SRA. SÁNCHEZ	3, 4	Yo voy a tomar *salpicón de marisco* y después *pimientos a la Riojana.*
• SR. SÁNCHEZ	5	Y a mí tráigame *gazpacho* y cordero asado.
CAMARERO		¿El cordero lo quiere con patatas o con ensalada?
• SR. SÁNCHEZ	6	Con patatas. Pero tráigame aparte una *ensalada mixta.*

CAMARERO		Bien. Y ¿para beber?
• SR. SÁNCHEZ	7	Un vino tinto de la región y una botella de *agua mineral sin gas*.

. . . .

CAMARERO	¿Van a tomar algo de postre?
SRA. SÁNCHEZ	Sí. Yo voy a tomar un flan.
• SR. SÁNCHEZ	Yo quiero tarta. ¿De qué la tienen?
CAMARERO	Pues, la hay de chocolate, de manzana, de almendras . . .
• SR. SÁNCHEZ	De almendras, por favor.
CAMARERO	¿Desean Vds. café?
SRA. SÁNCHEZ	No. A mí tráigame Vd. un té con leche.
• SR. SÁNCHEZ	8 A mí, un café solo y un coñac. Y cuando pueda deme Vd. *la cuenta*, por favor.
CAMARERO	Sí, señor. En seguida.

Explicaciones

1   En casi todos los restaurantes ofrecen el cubierto del día, compuesto de dos platos, postre, pan y en algunos casos vino, que resulta mas económico que la comida a la carta.

2   Fabada es un plato que se compone de judías blancas, chorizo, morcilla y rabo de buey.

3   Salpicón de marisco lleva gambas, langostinos, y trozos de langosta en un lecho de lechuga con salsa vinagreta o mayonesa.

4   Pimientos a la Riojana son pimientos rojos, rellenos de carne picada con una salsa de pimentón.

5   Gazpacho es una sopa fría que se hace con tomate, pimiento, pepino, cebolla, pan, aceite y vinagre.

6   Ensalada Mixta se compone de lechuga, tomate, cebolla y aceitunas.

7   Existen varias marcas de agua mineral con y sin gas.

8   Es costumbre dejar una propina equivalente al 10% del total de la cuenta.

Notes

1 In almost every restaurant you will be offered a set menu which comprises two courses, dessert, bread and (in some cases) wine. It is cheaper than the à la carte meal.

2 *Fabada* is a dish made with haricot beans, sausage, black pudding and ox tail.

3 *Salpicón de marisco* is a sea food salad consisting of certain varieties of prawns and pieces of lobster on a bed of lettuce, covered with a sauce vinagrette or with mayonnaise.

4 *Pimientos a la Riojana* are red peppers stuffed with minced meat in a paprika sauce.

5 *Gazpacho* is a cold soup made with tomatoes, peppers, cucumber, onion, bread, oil and vinegar.

6 *Ensalada mixta* is a salad made with lettuce, tomatoes, onion and olives.

7 There are many different mineral waters available, either sparkling or still.

8 It is customary to leave a tip of about 10% of the total cost of the meal.

En la panadería

• SRA. DIAZ	Buenos días.
PANADERO	Buenos días, señora. ¿Qué desea?
• SRA. DIAZ	¿Tiene Vd. pan de molde?
PANADERO	No, señora. No nos queda. Hasta mañana no lo tendremos. ¿Lo quiere para tostar?
• SRA. DIAZ	Sí.
PANADERO	1 Entonces, ¿por qué no se lleva. Vd. *pan bombón*? Está recién salido del horno.
• SRA. DIAZ	Bueno. Déme tres. Y déme también dos barras de cuarto de kilo.
PANADERO	Aqui tiene Vd. ¿Quiere algo más?
• SRA. DIAZ	2 Pues sí. Un paquete de *galletas* y dos *bollos suizos.* Y ¿tiene Vd. pan de centeno?
PANADERO	Sí, en barras. ¿Cuántas desea?
• SRA. DIAZ	3 Una, por favor. ¿Se endurecerá *si no la comemos hoy*?
PANADERO	No, señora. Le dura tres o cuatro días tierno.
• SRA. DIAZ	Entonces, déme Vd. dos. ¿Qué le debo?
PANADERO	Son ciento setenta y seis pesetas.
• SRA. DIAZ	Le doy doscientas una y así me devuelve Vd. veinticinco.
PANADERO	Se lo agradezco porque andamos muy mal de monedas de peseta.
• SRA. DIAZ	Adiós y gracias.
PANADERO	Adiós, señora.

Explicaciones

1 El pan bombón es una clase de panecillo, de blando, bueno para tostar, muy adecuado para desayunos y meriendas.

2 En casi todas las panaderías venden galletas y bollos, pero para comprar pasteles, tartas, bombones y caramelos hay que ir a una pastelería.

3 Las panaderías están abiertas los domingos por la mañana desde las ocho hasta la una.

Notes

1 *Pan bombón* is a kind of soft roll, suitable for toasting and very popular for breakfast and tea.

2 In most bakers' shops they sell biscuits and buns, but if one wants to buy cakes, gateaux, chocolates or sweets one has to go to a *pastelería*. *Bollos suizos* are the nearest Spanish equivalent to Bath buns.

3 Bakers' shops are open on Sunday mornings from 8 a.m. to 1 p.m.

En el estanco [1]

• CLIENTE	Buenas tardes. ¿Puede Vd. decirme cuánto es el franqueo para Inglaterra?
ESTANQUERA	Las cartas diecinueve pesetas, las postales doce pesetas.
• CLIENTE	Pues déme tres sellos de diecinueve pesetas y seis de doce.
ESTANQUERA	No me quedan sellos de diecinueve pesetas. Tendré que darle nueve de doce y tres de siete.
• CLIENTE	Está bien. No importa. También quiero elegir unas postales, ¿a cómo son?
ESTANQUERA	A siete pesetas cada una.
• CLIENTE	Me llevo estas seis. ¿Tiene Vd. puros habanos?
ESTANQUERA	Sí, señor. ¿Qué marca desea?
• CLIENTE	No sé. No entiendo mucho de puros. Son para un regalo. ¿Cuáles me recomienda?
ESTANQUERA	Estos son muy buenos. La caja de veinticinco puros vale mil ochocientas setenta y cinco pesetas. O los puede Vd. comprar sueltos a setenta y cinco pesetas cada uno.
• CLIENTE	¿No tiene Vd. nada más barato?
ESTANQUERA	Sí. Hay esta otra caja que cuesta mil quinientas. A sesenta pesetas cada puro.
• CLIENTE	Bueno. Entonces, me llevo esta caja. ¿Cuánto le debo en total?

ESTANQUERA	A ver, ¿qué lleva Vd? Los sellos, las postales y los puros . . . mil seiscientas setenta y una pesetas.
• CLIENTE	¿Puede Vd. cambiarme un billete de cinco mil?
ESTANQUERA	Sí, señor. Aquí tiene Vd. su cambio, tres mil trescientas veintinueve pesetas.
• CLIENTE	Muy bien. Gracias.
ESTANQUERA	Gracias, señor.

Explicaciones

1   Los estancos son establecimientos con licencia del Estado para vender tabaco, cerillas, sellos de correos y en algunos casos, lotería nacional. En la mayoría de ellos venden también tarjetas postales, papel de cartas, sobres, bolígrafos, etc.

Notes

1   *Estancos* are shops licensed to sell Government-controlled goods such as tobacco, matches, postage stamps and, in some cases, National Lottery tickets. In most of them one can also buy postcards, notepaper, envelopes, ballpoint pens, etc.

En la tienda de comestibles

• SRA. SÁNCHEZ		Buenos días.
TENDERO		Buenos días, señora.
• SRA. SÁNCHEZ	1	¿Tiene Vd. *jamón de York*?
TENDERO		Sí, señora. ¿Cuánto le pongo?
• SRA. SÁNCHEZ		Póngame cuarto de kilo en lonchas finas y déme también ciento cincuenta gramos de ese salchichón.
TENDERO		¿Algo más?
• SRA. SÁNCHEZ		¿Qué quesos tiene Vd.?
TENDERO	2 3	Pues tenemos *queso manchego*, de cabra, Gruyère y también *queso de Burgos* muy bueno.
• SRA. SÁNCHEZ	4	Póngame cuarto de queso manchego y cuarto de Burgos, y también un paquete de mantequilla de cien gramos, sin sal, una *botella de litro de leche descremada* y una docena de huevos.
TENDERO		Los huevos están en ese estante detrás de Vd. Cójalos, por favor. ¿Alguna cosa más?
• SRA. SÁNCHEZ		Necesito otra cosa y no recuerdo qué es.
TENDERO	5	¿Aceite, azúcar, *mermelada*?
• SRA. SÁNCHEZ		No . . . ya sé, un bote de tomate.
TENDERO		¿Al natural o frito?
• SRA. SÁNCHEZ		Al natural. Pero, ¿no lo hay más grande?

19

TENDERO	No, señora. En este momento sólo tengo este tamaño. Llévese Vd. dos.
● SRA. SÁNCHEZ	Bien. Déme Vd. dos. Voy a necesitar una bolsa porque no me cabe todo en la que tengo.
TENDERO	Sí, señora. Ahora mismo le doy una. Aquí tiene Vd.
● SRA. SÁNCHEZ	Gracias. ¿Qué le debo?
TENDERO	Son seiscientas diez.
● SRA. SÁNCHEZ	Tome Vd.
TENDERO	Gracias, señora. Adiós.
● SRA. SÁNCHEZ	Adiós.

Explicaciones

1 En España se vende jamón de York, que es jamón cocido con muy poca sal; jamón en dulce, que es jamón cocido con azúcar y jamón serrano que es jamón bien salado y curado.

2 El queso manchego es un queso de la región de La Mancha. Se hace con leche de oveja. Su sabor más o menos fuerte depende de su grado de curación.

3 El queso de Burgos es un queso cremoso, fresco, de consumo diario. Lleva el nombre de la región de la que proviene.

4 La leche se vende en botellas de litro y medio, y puede ser descremada o normal (con toda su crema).

5 La palabra mermelada se emplea para describir cualquier confitura de fruta.

Notes

1 In Spain one can buy *jamón de York* which is boiled ham with very little salt; *jamón en dulce* is ham boiled with sugar, and *jamón serrano* is ham that has been well salted and cured.

2 *Queso manchego* is a cheese from the region of La Mancha, made with ewe's milk. The strength of its flavour depends upon the degree of its maturity.

3 *Queso de Burgos* is a creamy, soft cheese which should be eaten within a day of purchase. It bears the name of the region from which it originated.

4 Milk is sold in bottles of 1 or 1½ litres. It can be skimmed or normal (full cream).

5 The word *mermelada* is used to describe both jam and marmalade.

En la carretera

(a) la estación de servicio

EMPLEADO	1	Buenos días. *¿Qué gasolina le pongo?*
• CLIENTE		Póngame Vd. mil pesetas de extra.
EMPLEADO		¿Puede Vd. mover el coche un poquito hacia delante? La manga del surtidor no llega al tanque.
• CLIENTE		Haga el favor de comprobar el aceite también.
EMPLEADO		Sí, señor, en seguida. Está un poco bajo.
• CLIENTE		Sí, eso me parecía. Ponga medio litro, por favor, y déme una lata pequeña para llevarme. ¿Me deja Vd. esa esponja para limpiar el parabrisas?
EMPLEADO		Sí, no faltaba más. Cójala.
• CLIENTE		Gracias. He tenido un pinchazo a unos kilómetros de aquí. ¿Hacen Vds. reparaciones?
EMPLEADO		Sí, vaya al taller que está allí enfrente y se lo arreglarán.
• CLIENTE		Muy bien.

(b) el taller de reparaciones

• CLIENTE	Buenos días. ¿Pueden Vds. arreglarme este pinchazo?
MECANICO	En este momento estamos muy ocupados. Tendrá Vd. que esperar.
• CLIENTE	¿Cuánto va a tardar?

MECANICO	Pues una hora aproximadamente.
• CLIENTE	¡Una hora! ¡Con la prisa que tengo! Tengo que llegar a Madrid antes de las siete. ¿A que distancia está la próxima estación de servicio?
MECANICO	A veinticinco kilómetros, pero no tienen taller de reparaciones. No es más que una gasolinera. Deje Vd. el neumático y trataré de hacérselo lo más rápidamente que pueda. Venga Vd. dentro de media hora.
• CLIENTE	Bien, gracias. Hasta ahora, entonces.

Explicaciones

1 En España hay tres clases de gasolina: normal de noventa octanos, super de noventa y seis octanos y extra de noventa y ocho octanos.

Notes

1 In Spain there are three kinds of petrol: *Normal* (90-octane) equivalent to the British 2-star, *super* (96-octane) equivalent to 3-star and *extra* (98-octane) equivalent to 4-star.

En la zapatería

DEPENDIENTA		Buenas tardes, señora.
• CLIENTE		Quisiera probarme unos zapatos de charol que he visto en el escaparate.
DEPENDIENTA		¿Quiere Vd. indicarme cuáles son?
• CLIENTE		Esos de dos mil ochocientas de hebilla.
DEPENDIENTA	1	Siéntese, por favor. ¿Qué *número* calza Vd.?
• CLIENTE		El treinta y siete.
DEPENDIENTA		Vamos a ver. ¿Le están cómodos?
• CLIENTE		No. Me aprietan mucho los dedos y el tacón es un poco alto. Me ha dado Vd. un treinta y siete ¿verdad?
DEPENDIENTA		Sí, es un treinta y siete. Es que es una horma muy estrecha y Vd. tiene el pie un poco ancho. Tengo otro modelo muy parecido de horma más ancha y tacón mas bajo, pero en tafilete, no en charol. ¿Quiere Vd. verlo?
• CLIENTE		Sí, haga el favor de enseñármelo.
DEPENDIENTA		Mire, a ver como le están estos. Como son de tafilete son más flexibles que los de charol.
• CLIENTE		Sí. Éstos me están mucho más cómodos. Y ¿son del mismo precio?
DEPENDIENTA		Sí, exactamente igual. Dos mil ocho cientas.
• CLIENTE		Entonces me los llevo. También quería ver unas zapatillas de lona, para la playa.

DEPENDIENTA	¿De qué color las quería? Las hay en azul marino, rojo y verde.
• CLIENTE	Enséñemelas en azul marino, por favor.
DEPENDIENTA	Tendrá que ponérselas con el calzador porque están un poquito fuertes, pero dan de si en cuanto se empieza a usarlas.
• CLIENTE	¿Qué precio tienen?
DEPENDIENTA	Setecientas cincuenta.
• CLIENTE	Pues me llevo dos pares. Uno en azul marino y otro en rojo.
DEPENDIENTA	¿Se lo pongo todo en una bolsa o quiere usted las cajas?
• CLIENTE	Prefiero una bolsa.
DEPENDIENTA	Muy bien. Pague en caja, por favor.

Explicaciones
1 Cuando hablamos de ropa utilizamos la palabra talla; para el calzado usamos la palabra número.

Notes
1 When talking of clothes use the word *talla*; to indicate size of footwear use the word *número*.

En la oficina de la RENFE [1]

• VIAJERO	2	Necesito dos billetes para Alicante para el día *veintiocho de este mes.* ¿Tiene Vd. algo?
EMPLEADA		¿En qué tren quería Vd. viajar?
• VIAJERO		¿Qué trenes hay?
EMPLEADA	3, 4	*El Talgo* que sale a las *quince cuarenta y ocho* y llega a las veinte cuarenta y
	5	cinco o *el Expreso* que sale a las veintidós cincuenta y seis y llega a las ocho de la mañana.
• VIAJERO		¿Lleva coche-cama el Expreso?
EMPLEADA		Sí, coche-cama y literas. Pero para esa fecha todas las camas están reservadas. Sólo quedan algunas literas. A finales de mes viaja mucha gente.
• VIAJERO		¡Qué lástima! Hubiera preferido viajar por la noche con este calor, pero quería cama, no me gustan las literas.
EMPLEADA		El Talgo tiene aire acondicionado, así que aunque viaje Vd. de día no va a pasar calor. Probablemente irá Vd. más fresco que en el Expreso. Y además el viaje en el Talgo es mucho más corto.
• VIAJERO		Bueno, entonces deme dos primeras de ida y vuelta para el Talgo. La vuelta para el día doce de agosto.
EMPLEADA		¡Vaya! Ha tenido Vd. suerte. No me quedan más que dos billetes para ese día.

• VIAJERO	¡Estupendo! ¿Cuánto le debo?
EMPLEADA	Nueve mil trescientas ochenta y cuatro.
• VIAJERO	Tome Vd. El tren sale de la Estación de Chamartín, ¿verdad?
EMPLEADA	Sí, señor. Y las horas de salida y llegada están impresas en los billetes.
• VIAJERO	Muy bien. Gracias.

Explicaciones

1 RENFE es la abreviatura de Red Nacional de Ferrocarriles Españoles.
2 En España es aconsejable sacar billetes de ferrocarril para viajes largos con anticipación, sobre todo durante los meses de verano.
3 El Talgo es un tren Diesel, rápido que lleva primera y segunda clase, aire acondicionado, servicio de bar y en viajes particularmente largos servicio de restaurant.
4 En los ferrocarriles españoles se usa el horario de veinticuatro horas.
5 El Expreso es un tren relativamente rápido que viaja por la noche y lleva primera y segunda clase, coche-cama y literas. En algunos viajes lleva también bar o coche restaurant.

Notes

1 RENFE stands for Spanish National Railways Network; pronounce it as one word.
2 In Spain it is advisable to book railway tickets for long journeys in advance, particularly during the summer months.
3 *Talgo* is a fast diesel train that has first and second class, air conditioning, bar and (on particularly long journeys) restaurant service.
4 Spanish railway timetables are based on the 24-hour clock.
5 *Expreso* is a comparatively fast night train that has first and second class, sleepers and couchettes. On certain journeys it also has a bar or a restaurant car.

En los grandes almacenes

(a) en la sección de confección de señora

DEPENDIENTA ¿La atienden, señora?

● CLIENTE No. ¿Podría probarme esta falda?

DEPENDIENTA Sí, señora. Pase Vd. al probador, allí enfrente.

● CLIENTE Gracias.

. . . .

● CLIENTE Me está un poco estrecha de cintura. ¿Tiene Vd. una talla más grande?

DEPENDIENTA A ver, ¿qué talla es ésta? La cuarenta y cuatro. Necesita Vd. la cuarenta y seis, pero en este color no la tenemos. Sólo nos queda esa talla en blanco y en rosa.

● CLIENTE ¡Qué lástima! Me gusta mucho èste tono de verde.

DEPENDIENTA Tenemos otras faldas en este mismo tono, pero no tienen tablas. ¿Quiere Vd. verlas?

● CLIENTE Sí, haga el favor de enseñármelas.

DEPENDIENTA Mire. Ésta tiene un corte muy bonito.

● CLIENTE Voy a probármela.

. . . .

DEPENDIENTA ¿Qué tal? ¿Le gusta?

● CLIENTE Sí, me está muy bien. Y creo que me sienta mejor este modelo que las tablas.

DEPENDIENTA	Sí, desde luego, le está a Vd. perfectamente. De todas formas si quiere Vd. probarse alguna otra...
• CLIENTE	No, me llevo ésta. No quiero molestarla más a Vd.
DEPENDIENTA	No es molestia, en absoluto, señora.
• CLIENTE	¿Tendría Vd. alguna blusa camisera, de manga larga que le fuera bien a este color?
DEPENDIENTA	Tengo ésta estampada. ¿Qué le parece?
• CLIENTE	Me gusta mucho, pero casi cuesta tanto como la falda. Es un poco cara. No tenía pensado gastarme tanto dinero.
DEPENDIENTA	Es que la calidad de las dos telas es buenísima. Tanto la falda como la blusa lavan maravillosamente. Y no necesitan plancha.
• CLIENTE	Bueno. Me ha convencido Vd. Me llevo las dos cosas.
DEPENDIENTA	1 Muy bien, señora. ¿Va Vd. a pagar con *tarjeta*?
• CLIENTE	No. En efectivo.
DEPENDIENTA	Entonces, haga el favor de acompañarme a la caja.
• CLIENTE	¿Puede decirme dónde está la sección de regalos?
DEPENDIENTA	En la planta baja.
• CLIENTE	Muchas gracias.
DEPENDIENTA	Gracias, señora.

(b) en la sección de regalos

DEPENDIENTE	2	Buenas *tardes*, señora. ¿Qué desea?

CLIENTE — Quisiera saber el precio de las figuras de porcelana de esta vitrina.

DEPENDIENTE — Pues mire, hay de muchos precios. Desde estas pequeñas a dos mil pesetas, hasta esta grande que vale doce mil quinientas. ¿Le gusta alguna?

• CLIENTE — Sí, aquella, ¿cuánto vale?

DEPENDIENTE — Esa, seis mil.

• CLIENTE — Es bonita, pero un poco cara.

DEPENDIENTE — ¿Cuánto quería Vd. gastarse?

• CLIENTE — Pues, no quería pasar de cuatro mil.

DEPENDIENTE — Mire. Esta vale tres mil quinientas.

• CLIENTE — No sé . . .

DEPENDIENTE — ¿Quiere Vd. ver alguna otra cosa? ¿Algún cacharro de cobre? Hay preciosidades y son más baratos.

• CLIENTE — Bueno. Si es Vd. tan amable.

DEPENDIENTE — Venga por aquí, por favor. Aquí tiene Vd. maceteros, candiles, ceniceros.

• CLIENTE — Este macetero me gusta. ¿Qué precio tiene?

DEPENDIENTE — Mil ochocientas.

• CLIENTE — ¡Ah! Entonces me lo llevo.

DEPENDIENTE	Muy bien, señora. ¿Quiere Vd. que se lo empaqueten para regalo?
• CLIENTE	Si es posible, sí, gracias. Y este abanico, ¿puede decirme lo que vale?
DEPENDIENTE	Ése, quinientas pesetas.
• CLIENTE	Me lo llevo también. ¿Pueden envolvérmelo como el macetero?
DEPENDIENTE	Desde luego, señora. Pague Vd. en caja y allí se lo prepararán.

Explicaciones
1 En algunos de los grandes almacenes se puede abrir una cuenta y pagar con la tarjeta expedida por ellos.
2 La mayoría de las tiendas cierran el sábado por la tarde.

Notes
1 In some of the large department stores one can open an account and pay with the card issued by them.
2 Most shops throughout Spain close on Saturday afternoons.

En la taquilla de la Plaza de Toros

• MR. JONES   1, 2   Buenos días. ¿Tiene Vd. entradas para *la corrida del domingo* que viene?

TAQUILLERO   Sí, señor, algunas quedan. ¿Qué entradas quería Vd?

• MR. JONES   No sé, porque no he estado nunca en una plaza de toros.

TAQUILLERO   3   Pues, mire Vd., hay la barrera que es *la más cara* y andanada que es la más barata. Entre medias están los tendidos. Yo le aconsejaría el tendido. Es una buena localidad desde la que se ve muy bien el ruedo.

• MR. JONES   Bien. Déme dos entradas de tendido.

TAQUILLERO   ¿Sol o sombra?

• MR. JONES   ¿Hay diferencia en el precio?

TAQUILLERO   Claro. Las entradas de sombra son más caras, pero merece la pena pagar la diferencia. ¿Quién quiere, estar sentado al sol con este calor?

• MR. JONES   Es verdad. Cogeré dos entradas de sombra. ¿A qué hora empieza la corrida?

TAQUILLERO   A las cinco en punto. Y procure Vd. no retrasarse, porque si llega Vd. cuando el toro ha salido ya al ruedo, no le dejan entrar hasta que le hayan matado.

- MR. JONES   Muy bien, gracias por la advertencia.

  TAQUILLERO   ¿Así que no ha visto Vd. nunca una corrida de toros? Pues espero que le guste.

- MR. JONES   Eso espero yo también. Adiós.

Explicaciones

1 La temporada de corridas de toros empieza en el mes de abril y acaba a últimos de septiembre. Las corridas suelen celebrarse en° domingo, pero hay corridas especiales que tienen lugar entre semana.

2 En las capitales grandes como Madrid, Barcelona o Sevilla hay corridas o novilladas todas las semanas durante la temporada. En las ciudades pequeñas y en los pueblos la temporada se reduce a unas cuantas corridas o novilladas durante las fiestas del lugar.

3 Los precios varían considerablemente. Depende de que sea una corrida o una novillada, del lugar donde se celebra y sobre todo de los toreros que tomen parte.

Notes

1 The bullfighting season begins in April and finishes at the end of September. Bullfights are usually held on Sunday, but there are special bullfights which take place on weekdays.

2 In the big capitals like Madrid, Barcelona or Seville there are bullfights every week during the season. In small towns and villages the season is limited to a few bullfights during the town or village festival.

3 The prices vary considerably, depending on whether it is a bullfight with mature bulls (*una corrida*) or a bullfight with young bulls (*una novillada*), on the place where it is held and, above all, on the bullfighters taking part.

Haciendo turismo

CONCHITA	¿Cuánto tiempo piensas pasar en Madrid, Robert?
• ROBERT	Diez días nada más, y quiero aprovecharlos, así que me gustaría que me aconsejaseis sobre las cosas de interés que puedo ver.
ALFONSO	Sí, no faltaba más. Y también te acompañaremos siempre que lo desees.
• ROBERT	¡Encantado! Como es mi primera visita a Madrid estoy bastante desorientado.
ALFONSO	Pues no te preocupes que mi mujer y yo te serviremos de guías, ¿verdad Conchita?
CONCHITA	Claro, será un placer.
• ROBERT	Este viaje es mitad vacación mitad negocios y mañana tengo que ver a unos clientes, pero el miércoles estaré libre.
ALFONSO	1 Entonces, ¿que te parece si vamos a *El Escorial*?
• ROBERT	Muy bien. En Inglaterra unos amigos míos me dijeron que no dejara de verlo.
CONCHITA	Es un edificio impresionante, emplazado en un lugar muy pintoresco. El pueblo es pequeño pero tiene mucho carácter.
• ROBERT	¿A qué distancia está de Madrid?
CONCHITA	A unos cuarenta y ocho kilómetros. Iremos en el autobús, ¿no crees tú Alfonso?

ALFONSO		Sí, se puede ir por tren también, pero la estación queda bastante lejos del Monasterio. Sin embargo el autobús nos deja muy cerca. Conchita, ¿sabes las horas de los autobuses?
CONCHITA		Sé que hay un autobús que sale a las nueve y media de la mañana. El viaje dura una hora, así que a las diez y media estamos en El Escorial. El autobús de vuelta creo que sale a las seis y media de modo que tenemos mucho tiempo para verlo todo con tranquilidad.
• ROBERT		Ese parece un plan muy bueno.
ALFONSO	2	Y ya que estamos en El Escorial podemos acercarnos al *Valle de los Caídos* que está sólo a unos pocos kilómetros. Hay autobuses desde El Escorial.
CONCHITA		¿Tú crees que nos dará tiempo a verlo?
ALFONSO		Yo creo que sí, si nos organizamos bien.
• ROBERT	3, 4	Bueno, entonces la excursión del miércoles está decidida. Otro día me gustaría ir al *Museo del Prado* y al *Palacio Real.*
ALFONSO		Los dos sitios están lo bastante cerca de aquí para poder ir andando. Ya te enseñaremos el camino. Pero, al Museo del Prado tendrás que ir varias veces si quieres verlo como es debido.
• ROBERT		Sí, ya me lo imagino. Tengo intención de pasar allí dos o tres mañanas. ¿Está abierto todos los días?
ALFONSO		Sí, incluso los domingos.

CONCHITA	Bueno, vas a estar muy ocupado toda esta semana, pero el domingo por la mañana me gustaría enseñarte El Rastro. Es un mercado al aire libre donde venden de todo. Desde animales domésticos hasta antigüedades.
ALFONSO	Es muy interesante y divertido. De vez en cuando se encuentra alguna ganga pero no muy a menudo.
• ROBERT	¡Ah! Eso me apetece mucho. Me encanta esa clase de mercado aunque no compre nada.
CONCHITA	Nosotros siempre que vamos acabamos comprando algo. A veces algo que realmente no necesitamos.
• ROBERT	Sí, ¡ese es el peligro! Los clientes que voy a ver mañana han ofrecido llevarme a Toledo un día de la semana que viene.
ALFONSO	Toledo es una ciudad maravillosa. Llena de historia y de tesoros artísticos. Te gustará muchísimo.
• ROBERT	Creo que mi estancia en Madrid desde el punto de vista turístico va a ser un éxito. Espero que mis negocios tengan el mismo éxito.
CONCHITA	Claro que lo tendrán. Todo te va a salir a las mil maravillas. Ya lo verás.

Explicaciones

1 El Real Monasterio de San Lorenzo de El Escorial fue construído por Felipe II para conmemorar la victoria de las tropas españoles en la batalla de San Quintín contra los franceses el día de San Lorenzo en el año 1557. Es un edificio inmenso de estilo Herreriano que ha sido Monasterio, Palacio y Panteón de los reyes de España desde Carlos I hasta Alfonso XIII.
Horas de visita:
Diario de 10 a 13 y de 15 a 18 (en invierno)
Diario de 10 a 13 y de 15 a 19 (en verano)

2 El Valle de los Caídos es un monumento a las victimas de la Guerra Civil Española de 1936. Tiene una basílica subterránea y una cruz de 150 metros de altura con un ascensor interior y una biblioteca en los brazos.
Horas de visita:
Diario de 9 a 18 (en invierno)
Diario de 9 a 19.30 (en verano)

3 El Museo del Prado es una de las galerías de arte más importantes del mundo. Construído en el siglo XVIII por Juan de Villanueva en el estilo Neoclásico, el Prado contiene una colección en la que la pintura española esta magníficamente representada y en la que se encuentran también numerosas e importantes obras de las escuelas flamenca, italiana y francesa.
Horas de visita:
Laborables de 10 a 17; Festivos de 10 a 14 (invierno)
Laborables de 10 a 18; Festivos de 10 a 14 (verano)

4 El Palacio Real también llamado Palacio de Oriente fue construído por los arquitectos Juvara y Sachetti en el siglo XVIII. Una gran parte del palacio está abierta al público y en el se pueden ver salas de diversos estilos, tapices e interesantes colecciones de cristal y porcelana. Hay también una Biblioteca y una Armería.
Horas de visita:
De 10 a 13 y de 15 a 18 (todo el año)

Notes

1 The *Real Monasterio de San Lorenzo de El Escorial* was built by Philip II to commemorate Spain's victory over the French in the battle of Saint Quentin, on St. Lawrence's Day 1557. It is a huge building in the Herreriano style which has been monastery, palace and mausoleum for the kings of Spain from Carlos I to Alfonso XIII.
Open daily from 10 a.m.-1 p.m. and 3 p.m.-6 p.m. (winter)
Open daily from 10 a.m.-1 p.m. and 3 p.m.-7 p.m. (summer)

2   The *Valle de los Caidos* is a war memorial to the fallen in the Spanish Civil War of 1936. It has an underground church and a cross 150 metres high with a lift inside and a library in its arms.
Open daily 9 a.m.-6 p.m. (winter)
Open daily 9 a.m.-7.30 p.m. (summer)

3   The *Prado* Museum is one of the most important art galleries in the world. Built in the 18th century by Juan de Villanueva in the Neo-Classical style, the Prado houses a collection in which Spanish painting is magnificently represented together with several important works of the Flemish, Italian and French Schools.
Open Monday to Saturday 10 a.m.-5 p.m. (winter)
Open Monday to Saturday 10 a.m. to 6 p.m. (summer)
Sundays & Public Holidays 10 a.m. 2 p.m. (all year)

4   The *Palacio Real* (also called *Palacio de Oriente*) was built by the architects Juvara and Sachetti in the 18th century. A large part of the Palace is open to the public and in it one can see rooms decorated in different styles, tapestries and some interesting collections of glass and porcelain. There is also a Library and an Armoury.
Open 10 a.m.-1 p.m. and 3 p.m.-6 p.m. (all year)

At the hotel

RECEPTION	Good morning sir. What can I do for you?
CLIENT	Good morning. Have you a single room for tonight?
RECEPTION	Just one night?
CLIENT	No, two nights.
RECEPTION	One moment, please, I am going to check. Yes, sir, I can offer you a room. Do you want one with a bathroom or with a shower?
CLIENT	What are the prices?
RECEPTION	The single room with a shower is one thousand eight hundred pesetas, with a bathroom it is two thousand five hundred.
CLIENT	Is breakfast included?
RECEPTION	Yes, sir, which room would you like?
CLIENT	I'll have the room with the shower.
RECEPTION	Fine. I can give you room 312 on the third floor. The lift is at the far end of the lobby. May I have your passport, please? I shall only keep it a few minutes.
CLIENT	There you are. Do they serve meals in the hotel?
RECEPTION	Yes, sir. We have a restaurant which is open from 1 p.m. to 4 p.m. and from 8 p.m. to 11 p.m. There is also a cafeteria open all day from 8 a.m. to midnight.

CLIENT	That's good; thanks.
RECEPTION	Have you any luggage?
CLIENT	Yes, in the car. I had to park it a block away because there was no room in front of the hotel.
RECEPTION	We have a garage, so you can bring the car and the porter will wait for you at the door to take your luggage.
CLIENT	Right, I'll go and fetch it now. Can you tell me if there is a bank near here? I need to change some money.
RECEPTION	You'll find a bank about five hundred yards from here. Turn right as you come out of the hotel. The bank is on the same side of the road.
CLIENT	All right, thank you. I'll be back in a little while.

In the café

CARMEN	Where shall we sit, at a table or at the bar?
PILAR	I think it is better at a table. The stools at the bar are not very comfortable.
CARMEN	That's true. Let's go to that table by the window.
WAITER	Good evening ladies. What would you like?
CARMEN	What can we eat?
WAITER	Pancakes, sandwiches, bocadillos, pepitos, hot dogs . . .
CARMEN	I'd like pancakes with cream, and a white coffee in a large cup.
WAITER	What would you like on your pancakes—maple syrup, chocolate sauce or strawberry syrup?
CARMEN	Maple syrup, please.
WAITER	And you madam, what are you going to have?
PILAR	I'll have a hot dog and a rum and coke.

. . . .

CARMEN	Where are the toilets, please?
WAITER	Through that door at the back.
CARMEN	Thank you. Is there a phone?
WAITER	Yes, next door to the toilets.
CARMEN	Can you change a hundred peseta note? I haven't any coins for the phone.

WAITER	Yes, madam. How would you like it?
CARMEN	Give me one fifty peseta coin, one twenty-five and the rest in fives if possible.
WAITER	There you are.
CARMEN	Thanks. Back in a minute, Pilar.
PILAR	All right!

At the restaurant

WAITER	Good morning, sir. A table for two? This way.
SR. SANCHEZ	While we choose, could you bring us a beer and a vermouth, please?
WAITER	Right away. Would you like anything to eat with it?
SR. SANCHEZ	Yes. Bring us some stuffed olives and some fried squid.
WAITER	Very good. Here is the menu. The set menu is very good. I can recommend it. It's fabada.
SR. SANCHEZ	(to his wife) What do you think? Shall we have the set menu?
SRA. SANCHEZ	I do not like the menu today. I prefer to eat à la carte.
SR. SANCHEZ	Yes, so do I.

. . . .

WAITER	Here are your aperitifs. Are you ready to order?
SRA. SANCHEZ	I am going to have a sea food salad and then peppers Riojana.
SR. SANCHEZ	I'd like gazpacho and roast lamb.
WAITER	Would you like the lamb with potatoes or with salad?
SR. SANCHEZ	With potatoes. But also bring me a mixed salad.
WAITER	Yes, sir. What are you going to drink?

42

SR. SANCHEZ	The local red wine and a bottle of mineral water.
	. . . .
WAITER	Would you like a dessert?
SRA. SANCHEZ	Yes. I'll have creme caramel.
SR. SANCHEZ	I'd like a slice of gateau. What have you got?
WAITER	There is chocolate, apple, or almond . . .
SR. SANCHEZ	I'll have the almond gateau, please.
WAITER	Are you going to have coffee?
SRA. SANCHEZ	No. I'll have tea with milk.
SR. SANCHEZ	For me a black coffee and a brandy. And will you give me the bill, please?
WAITER	Yes, sir. Right away.

At the baker's

SRA. DIAZ	Good morning.
BAKER	Good morning, madam. What would you like?
SRA. DIAZ	Have you a cut loaf?
BAKER	No, madam. We haven't any left. We won't have any until tomorrow. Did you want it for toast?
SRA. DIAZ	Yes.
BAKER	Why don't you take pan bombón, then? It has just come out of the oven.
SRA. DIAZ	All right. Give me three. And also give me two 250g baguette loaves.
BAKER	There you are. Anything else?
SRA. DIAZ	Yes, a packet of biscuits and two Bath buns. And, have you any rye bread?
BAKER	Yes, in baguette loaves. How many would you like?
SRA. DIAZ	One, please. Will it go stale if we don't eat it to-day?
BAKER	No, madam. It will stay fresh for three or four days.
SRA. DIAZ	In that case give me two. How much do I owe you?
BAKER	176 pesetas.
SRA. DIAZ	I'll give you 201 so that you can give me a 25 peseta coin back.
BAKER	I appreciate it because we haven't got many 1 peseta coins.
SRA. DIAZ	Thank you. 'Bye.
BAKER	Goodbye, madam.

At the tobacconist

CUSTOMER   Good afternoon. Can you tell me
                how much the postage to England
                is?

SHOPKEEPER   Letters are nineteen pesetas,
                postcards twelve.

CUSTOMER   Give me three 19 peseta stamps and
                six 12 peseta ones.

SHOPKEEPER   I haven't any 19 peseta stamps left.
                I'll have to give you nine twelves
                and three sevens.

CUSTOMER   That's all right, it doesn't matter. I
                also want to choose some postcards.
                How much are they?

SHOPKEEPER   Seven pesetas each.

CUSTOMER   I'll take six. Have you Havana
                cigars?

SHOPKEEPER   Yes, sir. Which make would you
                like?

CUSTOMER   I don't know. I don't know much
                about cigars. I want them for a
                present. Which ones would you
                recommend?

SHOPKEEPER   These are very good. The box with
                25 cigars is 1,875 pesetas. Or you
                can buy them loose at 75 pesetas
                each.

CUSTOMER   Haven't you anything cheaper?

SHOPKEEPER   Yes, there is this other box that
                costs 1,500 pesetas. 60 pesetas per
                cigar.

CUSTOMER	Well then, I'll take this box. How much do I owe you altogether?
SHOPKEEPER	Let's see, what have you got? The stamps, the postcards and the cigars . . . 1,671 pesetas.
CUSTOMER	Can you change a 5,000 peseta note?
SHOPKEEPER	Yes, sir. Here is your change, 3,329 pesetas.
CUSTOMER	Very good. Thank you.
SHOPKEEPER	Thank you, sir.

At the grocer's

SRA. SANCHEZ	Good morning.
SHOPKEEPER	Good morning, madam.
SRA. SANCHEZ	Have you boiled ham?
SHOPKEEPER	Yes, madam, how much would you like?
SRA. SANCHEZ	Give me a quarter of a kilo in thin slices and also a hundred and fifty grams of that salami.
SHOPKEEPER	Anything else?
SRA. SANCHEZ	What cheeses have you got?
SHOPKEEPER	We have manchego, goat's cheese, Gruyère and also Burgos cheese, very good.
SRA. SANCHEZ	I'll have a quarter of manchego and a quarter of Burgos, and also a hundred gram packet of unsalted butter, a litre of skimmed milk and a dozen eggs.
SHOPKEEPER	The eggs are on that shelf behind you. Will you take them, please? Anything else?
SRA. SANCHEZ	I need something else and I cannot remember what it is.
SHOPKEEPER	Cooking oil, sugar, jam?
SRA. SANCHEZ	No . . . I know, a tin of tomatoes.
SHOPKEEPER	Peeled tomatoes or purée?
SRA. SANCHEZ	Peeled. But haven't you got a bigger tin?
SHOPKEEPER	No, madam. Just now I have only this size. Why don't you take two?

SRA. SANCHEZ	All right, give me two tins. I am going to need a bag—I can't put everything in the one I have.
SHOPKEEPER	Yes, madam, I'll give you one. There you are.
SRA. SANCHEZ	Thank you. What do I owe you?
SHOPKEEPER	Six hundred and ten pesetas.
SRA. SANCHEZ	There you are.
SHOPKEEPER	Thank you, madam. Good bye.
SRA. SANCHEZ	Good bye.

On the road

(a) At the service station

ATTENDANT	Good morning. What kind of petrol do you want?
CUSTOMER	Give me 1,000 pesetas' worth of extra.
ATTENDANT	Could you move the car forward a little? The hose does not reach your tank.
CUSTOMER	Check the oil as well, please.
ATTENDANT	Yes, sir, straight away. It is a little low.
CUSTOMER	I thought so. Put in half a litre, please, and give me a small can to take with me. May I borrow that sponge to clean the windscreen?
ATTENDANT	Of course. Take it.
CUSTOMER	I had a puncture a few kilometres from here. Do you do repairs?
ATTENDANT	Yes, go to the repair workshop over there. They'll do it for you.
CUSTOMER	Very good.

(b) At the garage

CUSTOMER	Good morning. Can you repair this puncture for me?
MECHANIC	We are very busy just now. You'll have to wait.
CUSTOMER	How long will it take?

49

MECHANIC	About an hour.
CUSTOMER	An hour! I am in such a hurry! I have to be in Madrid before seven. What is the distance to the next garage?
MECHANIC	Twenty-five kilometres, but they don't do repairs. It's only a petrol station. Leave the tyre and I'll try to do it as soon as possible. Come back in half an hour.
CUSTOMER	All right, thanks. See you in a little while then.

At the shoe shop

ASSISTANT   Good afternoon, madam.

CUSTOMER   I'd like to try on a pair of patent leather shoes that I have seen in the window.

ASSISTANT   Could you show me which ones?

CUSTOMER   Those ones with the buckle that cost two thousand eight hundred.

ASSISTANT   Take a seat, please. What is your size?

CUSTOMER   37.

ASSISTANT   Let's see. Are they comfortable?

CUSTOMER   No. They are too tight in the front and the heel is a little high. This *is* a 37, isn't it?

ASSISTANT   Yes, it is 37. But it is a very narrow shoe and your foot is a little wide. I have another model, very similar, wider and with a lower heel, but in leather, not in patent leather. Would you like to see it?

CUSTOMER   Yes, please.

ASSISTANT   Look, let's try these on. Leather is more flexible than patent leather.

CUSTOMER   Yes, these are much more comfortable. And, are they the same price?

ASSISTANT   Yes, exactly the same. Two thousand eight hundred.

CUSTOMER   I'll take them then. I also wanted to look at some canvas shoes, for the beach.

ASSISTANT	What colour did you want? We have them in navy blue, red and green.
CUSTOMER	I'd like to see the navy blue ones, please.
ASSISTANT	You'll have to use the horn to put them on because they are a little stiff, but they stretch as soon as you start wearing them.
CUSTOMER	How much are they?
ASSISTANT	Seven hundred and fifty pesetas.
CUSTOMER	I'll take two pairs. One in navy blue and one in red.
ASSISTANT	Do you want them all in a bag or would you like the boxes?
CUSTOMER	I prefer a bag.
ASSISTANT	Very good. Pay at the cashier, please.

At the RENFE booking office

TRAVELLER	I need two tickets for Alicante for the 28th of this month. Have you anything?
CLERK	On which train do you wish to travel?
TRAVELLER	What trains are there?
CLERK	The Talgo which leaves at 15.48 and arrives at 20.45, or the Expreso that leaves at 22.56 and arrives at 8.00.
TRAVELLER	Does the Expreso have sleepers?
CLERK	Yes, sleepers and couchettes. But the sleepers are all booked for that date. There are only a few couchettes left. Many people travel at the end of the month.
TRAVELLER	What a pity! I would have preferred to travel overnight in this hot weather, but I wanted sleepers, I don't like couchettes.
CLERK	The Talgo has air conditioning, so even if you travel during the day you won't be hot. You will probably be cooler than in the Express. Besides, the journey in the Talgo is much shorter.
TRAVELLER	All right, give me two first class returns for the Talgo, coming back on the 12th of August.
CLERK	Well! You have been lucky. I have only two tickets left for that day.

TRAVELLER	Splendid! How much do I owe you?
CLERK	9,384 pesetas.
TRAVELLER	There you are. The train leaves from Chamartin Station, doesn't it?
CLERK	Yes, madam. And the times of departure and arrival are printed on the tickets.
TRAVELLER	Fine. Thank you.

At the department store

(a) in the ladies' clothes department

ASSISTANT	Are you being served, madam?
CUSTOMER	No. Could I try on this skirt?
ASSISTANT	Yes, madam. Go to the fitting room over there.
CUSTOMER	Thank you.

. . . .

	The waist is too small. Have you a bigger size?
ASSISTANT	Let me see, what size is this? 44. You need size 46 but we haven't got it in this colour. The only colours in that size are white and pink.
CUSTOMER	What a pity! I rather like this shade of green.
ASSISTANT	We have other skirts in this shade but they are not pleated. Would you like to see them?
CUSTOMER	Yes, please.
ASSISTANT	Look. This one has a very nice style.
CUSTOMER	I'll try it on.

. . . .

ASSISTANT	What do you think? Do you like it?
CUSTOMER	Yes, it fits me nicely. And I think this style suits me better than the pleats.
ASSISTANT	Yes, indeed, it is a perfect fit. Nevertheless, if you would like to try on any others . . .

CUSTOMER	No, I'll take this one. I don't want to trouble you any further.
ASSISTANT	It's no trouble at all, madam.
CUSTOMER	Would you have a shirt with long sleeves that would go well with this colour?
ASSISTANT	I have this one with a pattern. Do you like it?
CUSTOMER	I like it very much but it costs nearly as much as the skirt. It is a little expensive. I hadn't thought of spending so much money.
ASSISTANT	But the quality of both materials is very good. Both the skirt and the shirt wash beautifully. And they don't need ironing.
CUSTOMER	All right. You have convinced me. I'll take them both.
ASSISTANT	Very good, madam. Have you an account?
CUSTOMER	No, I am paying cash.
ASSISTANT	In that case, will you come with me to the cashier?
CUSTOMER	Can you tell me where the gift department is?
ASSISTANT	On the ground floor.
CUSTOMER	Thank you.
ASSISTANT	Thank you, madam.

(b)   in the gift department

ASSISTANT	Good afternoon, madam. Can I help you?
CUSTOMER	I'd like to know the price of the porcelain figures in this show-case.
ASSISTANT	Well, there are many prices. From 2,000 pesetas for these small ones to 12,500 for this big one. Do you like any of them?
CUSTOMER	Yes, that one. How much is it?
ASSISTANT	6,000.
CUSTOMER	It's beautiful, but too expensive.
ASSISTANT	How much did you want to spend?
CUSTOMER	I didn't want to go over 4,000.
ASSISTANT	Look. This one is 3,500.
CUSTOMER	I don't know . . .
ASSISTANT	Would you like to see anything else? Something made of copper? There are some very pretty things and they are cheaper.
CUSTOMER	All right. If you wouldn't mind.
ASSISTANT	Come this way, please. There are plant pot holders, oil lamps, ash trays.
CUSTOMER	I like this plant pot. What is the price?
ASSISTANT	1,800.
CUSTOMER	Oh! I'll take it then.
ASSISTANT	Very good, madam. Would you like to have it gift wrapped?
CUSTOMER	Yes, if it's possible, thanks. And this fan, how much is it?

ASSISTANT	That one is 500 pesetas.
CUSTOMER	I'll take it too. Can I have it wrapped the same as the plant pot?
ASSISTANT	Of course, madam. Pay at the cashier and they will wrap it all up for you there.

Buying tickets for the bullfight

MR. JONES   Good morning. Have you any tickets for next Sunday's bullfight?

CLERK   Yes, sir, there are some left. Where do you want to sit?

MR. JONES   I don't know because I have never been to a bullring.

CLERK   Well, there is *barrera* which is the most expensive seat and *andanada* which is the cheapest. In between there are the *tendidos*. I would recommend you take *tendido*. It is a good seat and you can see the ring very well.

MR. JONES   Fine. Give me two *tendidos*.

CLERK   In the sun or in the shade?

MR. JONES   Is there much difference in the price?

CLERK   Of course. The seats in the shade are more expensive, but it is well worth paying the difference. Who wants to sit in the sun in this heat?

MR. JONES   You are right. I'll have two seats in the shade. What time does the bullfight start?

CLERK   Five o'clock. Try to be punctual because if you arrive when the bull is already in the ring, they won't let you in until it has been killed.

MR. JONES   Very good. Thanks for the warning.

CLERK   So, you have never seen a bullfight? Well, I hope you like it.

MR. JONES   I hope so too. Good bye.

Sightseeing

CONCHITA	How long are you going to be in Madrid, Robert?
ROBERT	Only ten days, and I want to make the most of them, so I'd like you both to advise me on the interesting things I can see.
ALFONSO	Yes, of course. And we'll accompany you too whenever you wish.
ROBERT	Delighted! As it is my first visit to Madrid I am feeling rather lost.
ALFONSO	Well, don't worry. My wife and I will be your guides, won't we, Conchita?
CONCHITA	Of course, it will be a pleasure.
ROBERT	This trip is half holiday half business and tomorrow I have to see some clients, but I shall be free on Wednesday.
ALFONSO	In that case, shall we go to El Escorial?
ROBERT	Fine. Some friends of mine in England told me not to miss it.
CONCHITA	It is an impressive building, situated in a very picturesque spot. The town is small but it has great character.
ROBERT	How far is it from Madrid?
CONCHITA	About 48 kilometres. We'll go by bus, don't you think, Alfonso?

ALFONSO	Yes, one can also go by train, but the station is rather far from the Monastery. On the other hand the bus stops very near. Conchita, do you know the times of the buses?
CONCHITA	I know that there is a bus leaving at half past nine in the morning. The journey lasts an hour, so at half past ten we'll be in El Escorial. The return bus leaves at half past six I think, so we have plenty of time to see everything unhurriedly.
ROBERT	That seems a very good plan.
ALFONSO	And since we are at El Escorial, we can pay a visit to the Valle de los Caidos which is only a few kilometres away. There are buses from El Escorial.
CONCHITA	Do you think that we'll have time to see it?
ALFONSO	I think so, if we organise ourselves well.
ROBERT	All right then, the trip for Wednesday has been decided. Some other day I'd like to go to the Prado Museum and the Royal Palace.
ALFONSO	Both places are within walking distance. We'll show you the way. But you'll have to visit the Prado a few times if you want to see it properly.
ROBERT	Yes, I imagine so. I intend to spend two or three mornings there. Is it open every day?
ALFONSO	Yes, even on Sundays.

CONCHITA	Well, you are going to be very busy all this week, but on Sunday morning I should like to show you the Rastro. It is an open-air market where they sell all sorts of things, from pets to antiques.
ALFONSO	It is very interesting and amusing. One finds the occasional bargain, but not very often.
ROBERT	Oh! That appeals to me very much. I love that kind of market, even if I don't buy anything.
CONCHITA	We always end up buying something, whenever we go. Sometimes something that we don't really need.
ROBERT	Yes, that is the danger! The clients I have to see tomorrow have offered to take me to Toledo one day next week.
ALFONSO	Toledo is a wonderful city. Full of history and artistic treasures. You will like it very much.
ROBERT	I think that my stay in Madrid from the holiday point of view is going to be a success. I hope that my business will be just as successful.
CONCHITA	Of course it will. Everything is going to work out perfectly. You'll see.

Further publications from

hugo

The 'Three Months' series
Teach yourself a new language in three months using the famous Hugo method with easy imitated pronunciation.

Audio courses
The 'Three Months' books with cassettes, so you can hear the language as it is spoken.

The 'Speak Today' series
A cassette and a book for improving your colloquial ability in a foreign language.

Verb books
Invaluable reference books with complete lists of verbs, with their formation explained.

Travel packs
One phrase book with a cassette, so you can practise the phrases before your trip!

Phrase books
Useful phrases for all essential situations abroad, plus a menu guide and mini-dictionary.

Pocket dictionaries
Over 22,000 words in each, with imitated pronunciation.

Write to us for prices and more details, or phone (0728) 746546.
Hugo's Language Books Ltd., Old Station Yard, Marlesford, Woodbridge, Suffolk IP13 0AG.